The Power of Execution

Getting Big Things Done in Business.

Jorge Watson

Copyright message

Table of Contents

- Overcoming Mental Barriers to Achieve Big Things in
Business

Conclusion: The Power of Execution Unleashed

- Recap of Key Insights and Actionable Steps for Getting Big
Things Done in Business

Introduction: Unleashing the Power of Execution

In the fast-paced and ever-evolving world of business, ideas and strategies are abundant, but the ability to execute them effectively is what sets successful organizations apart. "The Power of Execution: Getting Big Things Done in Business" is a comprehensive guide that looks into the principles and strategies necessary for businesses to overcome the challenges of execution and achieve their most ambitious goals.

The premise of this book is simple yet profound: execution is the key element that separates thriving businesses from those that falter. While a clear vision and robust strategy are essential, it is the capacity to execute effectively that ultimately determines success. This book is designed to equip business leaders, managers, and entrepreneurs with practical insights and actionable steps to enhance their execution capabilities and drive their organizations toward success.

The first section of the book lays emphasis on the critical importance of execution in business. It explores how execution permeates every facet of an organization, from day-to-day operations to long-term strategic endeavors. Real-world examples of both successful and unsuccessful businesses underscore the important role that execution plays in realizing business objectives.

Moving forward, the book addresses the common challenges and barriers that impede effective execution within organizations. These obstacles may include issues such as poor communication, lack of accountability, ineffective resource allocation, and resistance to change. By identifying and understanding these challenges, readers will be better equipped to proactively address them within their own organizational contexts.

Subsequently, the book shifts its focus to practical strategies for improving execution. It provides guidance on setting clear and achievable goals, establishing robust accountability mechanisms, fostering a culture of execution, and leveraging technology and data to drive informed decision-making. The pivotal role of effective leadership in driving execution, as well as the significance of teamwork and collaboration in achieving substantial business outcomes, is also thoroughly explored.

Throughout the book, readers will encounter actionable tips, compelling case studies, and thought-provoking exercises designed to facilitate the application of concepts and strategies discussed. The goal is to provide a comprehensive roadmap for enhancing execution capabilities within any business setting.

As the book nears its conclusion, it transitions into a discussion on the future of execution in business. With technology continuously evolving and disrupting traditional business models, the ability to execute effectively is becoming increasingly critical. Emerging trends and best practices are explored to equip businesses with the tools needed to thrive in an intensely competitive and dynamic environment.

In summary, "The Power of Execution: Getting Big Things Done in Business" aims to empower readers with the knowledge and tools necessary to excel in execution. By mastering the principles and strategies outlined in this book, businesses can surmount the challenges of execution and achieve their most ambitious goals. Whether you are a seasoned business leader or an aspiring entrepreneur, this book offers valuable insights that can propel you toward success in today's competitive business landscape.

Are you ready to unleash the power of execution within your organization? "The Power of Execution: Getting Big Things Done in Business" provides a roadmap for transforming your business's potential into tangible results. Equip yourself with the knowledge and tools necessary to drive success in today's competitive business world. Join us on this transformative journey towards mastering execution and achieving your most ambitious goals!

Chapter 1: Business Strategy Success Stories

1.1 Case Studies of Companies Achieving Remarkable Results Through Strategic Execution.

In the business world, strategic execution is what separates thriving organizations from those that fail the test of time. In this chapter, we look into compelling case studies of companies that have achieved remarkable success through effective strategic execution. These stories serve as powerful testaments to the transformative impact of execution in realizing ambitious business goals.

One such exemplary case is that of Apple Inc., a company renowned for its innovative products and unwavering commitment to strategic execution. Under the visionary leadership of Steve Jobs, Apple executed a bold strategy that revolutionized multiple industries. The successful launch of the iPod, iPhone, and iPad exemplifies Apple's mastery of strategic execution, propelling the company to unprecedented levels of success and market dominance.

Similarly, Amazon's meteoric rise from an online bookstore to a global e-commerce behemoth stands as a testament to the power of strategic execution. Led by Jeff Bezos, Amazon executed a relentless strategy focused on customer-centric innovation, operational excellence, and strategic acquisitions. Through meticulous execution, Amazon has redefined consumer expectations, disrupted traditional retail paradigms, and diversified into diverse industries such as cloud computing and entertainment.

Another compelling case study is that of Netflix, a company that transformed the entertainment landscape through strategic execution. By pivoting from a DVD rental service to a streaming powerhouse, Netflix harnessed the power of strategic execution to anticipate market trends and capitalize on shifting consumer behaviors. Through original content production, global expansion, and data-driven personalization, Netflix's strategic execution has propelled it to the forefront of the entertainment industry.

Furthermore, the strategic execution prowess of Starbucks has been instrumental in its global success. By meticulously executing a strategy centered on customer experience, premiumization, and digital innovation, Starbucks has solidified its position as a leading global coffee chain. The company's ability to consistently execute its vision across thousands of stores worldwide underscores the transformative impact of strategic execution on organizational success.

These case studies underscore the pivotal role of strategic execution in driving business success. They highlight the importance of aligning vision with action, fostering a culture of innovation, and leveraging strategic agility to capitalize on market opportunities. Moreover, they emphasize the indispensable role of leadership in championing strategic execution and instilling a relentless focus on realizing organizational goals.

As we unravel these success stories, it becomes evident that strategic execution is not merely a theoretical concept but a tangible force that propels businesses to unparalleled heights. These companies serve as beacons of inspiration, demonstrating that with unwavering commitment to strategic execution, even the most audacious business aspirations can be transformed into reality.

In conclusion, the case studies presented in this chapter serve as compelling evidence of the transformative power of strategic execution in driving business success. By studying these success stories, business leaders and managers can glean valuable insights and inspiration to enhance their own organizations' execution capabilities. As we proceed through this book, we will probeprobe deeper into the principles and strategies that underpin effective strategic execution, empowering readers to emulate the success of these remarkable companies within their own organizational contexts.

1.2 Lessons Learned from Successful Business Strategies

The case studies of companies achieving remarkable success through strategic execution offer invaluable insights and lessons for business leaders seeking to emulate their achievements. These success stories underscore several key lessons that can serve as guiding principles for organizations striving to realize their strategic aspirations.

First and foremost, the importance of visionary leadership in driving strategic execution cannot be overstated. The success stories of Apple, Amazon, Netflix, and Starbucks are intrinsically linked to the visionary leadership of individuals such as Steve Jobs, Jeff Bezos, and Howard Schultz. These leaders demonstrated the ability to envision bold strategies, inspire their teams, and drive relentless execution towards ambitious goals. Their unwavering commitment to realizing a compelling vision serves as a powerful lesson in the pivotal role of leadership in shaping organizational success.

Moreover, the case studies highlight the significance of customer-centric innovation as a cornerstone of successful business strategies. Companies such as Apple and Amazon have consistently prioritized customer needs and preferences, leveraging strategic execution to deliver innovative products and services that resonate with their target audience. This customer-centric approach underscores the importance of aligning strategic initiatives with a deep understanding of customer behaviors, preferences, and evolving market trends.

Additionally, the transformative power of strategic flexibility emerges as a critical lesson from these success stories. The ability of companies such as Amazon and Netflix to pivot, adapt, and capitalize on emerging market opportunities exemplifies the importance of strategic agility in navigating complex business landscapes. These companies have demonstrated the capacity to swiftly adjust their strategies in response to changing market dynamics, technological disruptions, and evolving consumer demands, underscoring the imperative of flexibility in strategic execution.

Furthermore, the case studies emphasize the significance of fostering a culture of innovation and continuous improvement within organizations. Apple's relentless pursuit of groundbreaking products, Amazon's culture of experimentation, Netflix's commitment to original content production, and Starbucks' focus on elevating the customer experience all underscore the transformative impact of fostering a culture that encourages creativity, risk-taking, and relentless pursuit of excellence.

In conclusion, the lessons gleaned from the success stories of these companies provide a rich tapestry of insights for organizations seeking to enhance their strategic execution capabilities. By embracing visionary leadership, prioritizing customer-centric innovation, cultivating strategic agility, and fostering a culture of innovation, businesses can glean valuable lessons from these remarkable success stories to chart their own paths towards achieving remarkable results through strategic execution.

Chapter 2. Tactical Execution Roadmap

2.1 Developing a Comprehensive Plan for Executing Business Strategies.

In the fast-paced and competitive world of business, having a well-thought-out strategy is only half the battle. The other half lies in the execution of that strategy. Developing a comprehensive plan for executing business strategies is essential for ensuring that the strategic vision is effectively translated into tangible results. When and how a company develops and implements this plan can make all the difference in achieving success.

Timing is crucial when it comes to developing a plan for executing business strategies. Ideally, this process should begin as soon as the overall business strategy is formulated. By aligning the execution plan with the strategic vision from the outset, companies can ensure that their efforts are focused and coordinated. However, it's never too late to develop an execution plan. Even if a strategy is already in place, it's important to assess whether the current approach is yielding the desired results and adjust the execution plan accordingly.

The first step in developing a comprehensive plan for executing business strategies is to clearly **define the objectives and goals of the strategy**. This involves breaking down the overarching strategic vision into specific, measurable targets that can guide the execution process. These goals should be aligned with the company's overall mission and vision, and should be realistic and achievable within a given timeframe.

Once the objectives are established, the next step is to **identify the key initiatives and actions required to achieve those goals**. This involves a thorough analysis of the resources, capabilities, and potential obstacles that may impact the execution of the strategy. It's important to consider factors such as market conditions, competitive landscape, internal capabilities, and external risks when formulating these initiatives.

Another critical aspect of developing an execution plan is to **allocate resources effectively**. This includes not only financial resources but also human capital, technology, and time. Companies need to ensure that they have the right people with the right skills in place to drive the execution process. Additionally, technology and infrastructure should support the initiatives outlined in the plan.

Communication and alignment are also key components of a successful execution plan. It's essential to ensure that everyone within the organization understands their role in executing the strategy and is aligned with the overall objectives. Clear communication channels and regular updates on progress are vital to keep everyone focused and motivated.

Finally, monitoring and adapting the plan as needed is crucial for successful execution. Regular assessment of progress against the set goals allows for adjustments to be made in response to changing circumstances or unexpected challenges.

In conclusion, developing a comprehensive plan for executing business strategies is a critical step in turning strategic visions into reality. By carefully defining objectives, identifying key initiatives, allocating resources effectively, ensuring alignment, and monitoring progress, companies can maximize their chances of success. Whether at the outset of a new strategy or in response to ongoing challenges, creating and implementing an effective execution plan is essential for achieving business objectives.

2.2 Implementing Effective Tactics to Achieve Business Goals

In the dynamic landscape of business, setting ambitious goals is just the beginning. The real challenge lies in implementing effective tactics to achieve those goals. By strategically planning and executing these tactics, businesses can propel themselves towards success and growth. Here are some unique and attractive tactics to achieve business goals and how to implement them.

1. **Data-Driven Decision Making**:
Utilizing data to drive decision making is a powerful tactic for achieving business goals. By analyzing customer behavior, market trends, and internal performance metrics, businesses can make informed decisions that lead to tangible results. Implementing this tactic involves investing in data analytics tools, training employees on data interpretation, and creating a culture that values data-driven insights.

2. **Agile Project Management:**
Adopting agile project management methodologies can significantly enhance a company's ability to achieve its goals. This approach emphasizes flexibility, collaboration, and iterative progress, allowing teams to adapt quickly to changing circumstances. Implementing agile project management involves training teams on agile principles, establishing cross-functional collaboration, and using digital tools to facilitate agile workflows.

3. **Customer-Centric Innovation**:
Focusing on customer needs and preferences is a powerful tactic for driving business growth. By prioritizing customer-centric innovation, businesses can create products and services that truly resonate with their target audience. Implementing this tactic involves conducting in-depth market research, gathering customer feedback, and empowering cross-functional teams to ideate and implement customer-centric solutions.

4. **Strategic Partnerships:**

Forming strategic partnerships with other businesses can open up new opportunities for achieving business goals. Whether through joint ventures, co-marketing initiatives, or supplier collaborations, strategic partnerships can provide access to new markets, resources, and expertise. Implementing this tactic involves identifying potential partners, negotiating mutually beneficial agreements, and establishing clear communication channels.

5. **Employee Empowerment**:

Empowering employees to take ownership of their work and contribute innovative ideas is a tactic that can drive business success. By fostering a culture of empowerment and autonomy, businesses can tap into the full potential of their workforce. Implementing this tactic involves providing training and development opportunities, soliciting employee input on decision-making processes, and recognizing and rewarding initiative-taking.

6. **Technology Integration:**

Integrating cutting-edge technologies into business processes is a tactic that can enhance efficiency and productivity. Whether through automation, artificial intelligence, or advanced analytics, technology integration can streamline operations and drive strategic outcomes. Implementing this tactic involves assessing technology needs, investing in relevant tools and systems, and providing training to ensure seamless adoption.

To implement these tactics effectively, businesses should start by clearly defining their goals and aligning their tactics with those objectives. It's essential to allocate resources appropriately, communicate the strategy effectively throughout the organization, and regularly monitor progress to make adjustments as needed.

In conclusion, implementing effective tactics to achieve business goals requires a combination of strategic thinking, resource allocation, and effective execution. By embracing data-driven decision making, agile project management, customer-centric innovation, strategic partnerships, employee empowerment, and technology integration, businesses can position themselves for success in a competitive marketplace.

Chapter 3. Leadership Insights for Results

3.1 The Role of Leadership in Driving Successful Execution

In the ever-evolving landscape of business, the role of leadership in driving successful execution cannot be overstated. Effective leadership is the catalyst that transforms vision into reality, strategy into action, and goals into tangible results. It encompasses the ability to inspire, guide, and empower teams to achieve their full potential and deliver exceptional outcomes. Let's delve into the key aspects of leadership that are instrumental in driving successful execution.

1. **Visionary Guidance:**
Leadership plays a pivotal role in articulating a compelling vision that inspires and aligns the entire organization. A clear and ambitious vision serves as a guiding light, providing a sense of purpose and direction for employees. By effectively communicating the vision, leaders can instill a shared sense of mission, motivating teams to rally behind common goals and drive successful execution.

2. **Strategic Alignment:**
Successful execution hinges on strategic alignment, ensuring that every initiative and effort is synchronized

with overarching business objectives. Leaders must adeptly align resources, capabilities, and efforts towards the fulfillment of strategic goals. This involves creating a cohesive framework that connects individual tasks to the broader organizational strategy, fostering a unified approach to execution.

3. **Empowerment and Accountability**:
Empowering employees to take ownership of their work and holding them accountable for results are essential leadership responsibilities. Effective leaders create an environment where individuals are empowered to make decisions, take calculated risks, and innovate. Simultaneously, they establish clear accountability mechanisms, setting performance expectations and providing constructive feedback to ensure that execution stays on track.

4. **Adaptability and Resilience:**
In today's fast-paced business environment, adaptability and resilience are critical attributes for successful execution. Leaders must navigate through uncertainty, rapid changes, and unforeseen challenges with agility and composure. By fostering a culture of adaptability and resilience, leaders enable their teams to pivot when necessary, learn from setbacks, and persevere in the pursuit of goals.

5. **Inspirational Motivation:**
Leadership that drives successful execution is characterized by inspirational motivation. Effective

leaders inspire commitment and dedication by fostering a positive and motivational work environment. They recognize and celebrate achievements, provide encouragement during tough times, and lead by example, instilling confidence and enthusiasm in their teams.

6. **Continuous Improvement:**
Leadership's role in driving successful execution extends to promoting a culture of continuous improvement. Leaders encourage a mindset of learning, experimentation, and refinement, fostering an environment where teams strive for excellence and seek opportunities for growth and innovation.

In conclusion, the role of leadership in driving successful execution is multifaceted and indispensable. Visionary guidance, strategic alignment, empowerment, adaptability, inspirational motivation, and a commitment to continuous improvement are all essential components of effective leadership in achieving successful execution. When leaders embody these traits and principles, they pave the way for their organizations to realize their full potential and achieve sustainable success.

3.2. Inspiring and Motivating Teams to Execute with Excellence

In the pursuit of achieving targeted goals, inspiring and motivating teams to execute with excellence is a critical responsibility for leaders. It is the driving force that propels organizations towards success and enables them to surpass their objectives. Here are some unique and compelling insights on how leaders can inspire and motivate their teams to execute with excellence, ultimately achieving their targeted goals.

1. **Cultivate a Compelling Vision:**
A compelling vision serves as a powerful source of inspiration for teams. Leaders should articulate a vision that ignites passion and purpose, painting a vivid picture of the desired future state. By communicating a clear and ambitious vision, leaders instill a sense of direction and meaning, fueling the motivation of their teams to strive for excellence in execution.

2. **Foster a Culture of Trust and Collaboration**:
Trust and collaboration form the bedrock of a motivated and high-performing team. Leaders should prioritize building trust among team members, fostering an environment where open communication, respect, and mutual support are valued. When individuals feel trusted and connected, they are more inclined to collaborate seamlessly, share ideas, and work cohesively towards achieving common goals.

3. **Provide Meaningful Recognition and Rewards**:
Recognition and rewards are potent motivators that fuel a team's commitment to executing with excellence. Leaders should actively acknowledge and celebrate the achievements and contributions of their team members. Whether through public praise, bonuses, or career development opportunities, meaningful recognition and rewards reinforce a culture of excellence and inspire teams to consistently deliver outstanding results.

4. **Encourage Autonomy and Innovation:**
Empowering teams to make decisio hins and innovate fosters a sense of ownership and creativity. Leaders should provide autonomy for individuals to explore new ideas, experiment with solutions, and take calculated risks. By encouraging a culture of innovation, leaders inspire teams to push boundaries, think outside the box, and execute with excellence in pursuit of innovative solutions.

5. **Lead by Example:**
Leaders who lead by example set the standard for excellence in execution. By demonstrating dedication, resilience, and a commitment to high standards, leaders inspire their teams to emulate their behavior. When leaders consistently exhibit a strong work ethic, integrity, and a positive attitude, they motivate their teams to uphold similar values and strive for excellence in their own endeavors.

6. **Foster Personal Growth and Development:**
Investing in the personal growth and development of team members demonstrates a commitment to their well-being and professional advancement. Leaders should provide opportunities for skill development, mentorship, and career progression. By nurturing the growth of individuals within the team, leaders inspire a sense of purpose and motivation, driving them to execute with excellence in pursuit of their personal and professional aspirations.

In conclusion, inspiring and motivating teams to execute with excellence is a transformative leadership imperative that fuels organizational success. By cultivating a compelling vision, fostering trust and collaboration, providing meaningful recognition, encouraging autonomy and innovation, leading by example, and fostering personal growth, leaders can create an environment where teams are inspired to execute with unwavering excellence, ultimately achieving their targeted goals.

Chapter 4. Proven Business Implementation Tactics

4.1 Practical Approaches for Implementing Business Strategies

Implementing business strategies is a pivotal stage in the journey towards achieving organizational goals and objectives. It requires a systematic and well-executed approach to ensure that strategies are effectively translated into tangible actions and results. Here are unique and practical approaches for implementing business strategies that drive success and sustainable growth.

1. Develop a Detailed Implementation Plan:
A comprehensive implementation plan serves as a roadmap for executing business strategies. It should outline specific action steps, responsibilities, timelines, and key performance indicators (KPIs) to track progress. By clearly defining the who, what, when, and how of implementation, organizations can ensure alignment and accountability across teams, facilitating a smooth and coordinated execution of strategies.

2. Communicate and Cascade Strategy Throughout the Organization:
Effective communication is essential for ensuring that every member of the organization understands the strategic direction and their role in its implementation. Leaders should communicate the strategy clearly and consistently across all levels of the organization, cascading it down to individual teams and employees. This approach creates a shared understanding of the strategic priorities and fosters alignment towards common goals.

3. Align Resources and Capabilities:
Successful strategy implementation hinges on aligning resources, capabilities, and processes with the strategic objectives. Leaders should assess the organization's existing resources, including human capital, technology, and financial assets, to determine if they are aligned with the strategic requirements. By identifying and addressing resource gaps, organizations can ensure that they have the necessary tools and capabilities to execute the strategy effectively.

4. Foster a Culture of Adaptability and Agility:
In today's dynamic business environment, adaptability and agility are critical for successful strategy implementation. Organizations should foster a culture that embraces change, encourages innovation, and responds swiftly to market dynamics. By promoting adaptability, organizations can proactively adjust their implementation approach in response to evolving

conditions, ensuring that strategies remain relevant and effective.

5. **Establish Clear Accountability and Performance Metrics:**

Clear accountability is essential for driving ownership and commitment to strategy implementation. Leaders should define clear roles and responsibilities for each team member involved in the implementation process. Additionally, establishing performance metrics and regular progress reviews enables organizations to monitor the effectiveness of implementation efforts, identify bottlenecks, and make informed adjustments to stay on course.

6. **Continuously Monitor and Adapt Implementation Efforts:**

Continuous monitoring and adaptation are fundamental to successful strategy implementation. Organizations should establish mechanisms for ongoing performance measurement, feedback collection, and learning from implementation experiences. This iterative approach allows organizations to identify areas for improvement, capitalize on successes, and adapt their implementation tactics to optimize outcomes.

7. **Celebrate Milestones and Learn from Setbacks**:

Recognizing and celebrating milestones achieved during strategy implementation fosters a sense of accomplishment and motivation within the organization. Equally important is learning from setbacks or obstacles encountered along the way. Organizations should view setbacks as opportunities for learning and improvement, leveraging these experiences to refine their implementation tactics and strengthen their ability to overcome future challenges.

In conclusion, implementing business strategies requires a holistic and disciplined approach that encompasses detailed planning, effective communication, resource alignment, adaptability, clear accountability, continuous monitoring, and a culture of learning. By embracing these practical approaches, organizations can enhance their capacity to translate strategic intent into impactful actions, driving sustainable business success.

4.2 Overcoming Challenges and Obstacles in Execution: The Best Approach

In both personal and professional endeavors, challenges and obstacles are inevitable. Whether it's launching a new project, pursuing a career change, or striving to achieve a long-term goal, the path to success is often riddled with roadblocks. However, it's not the presence of these obstacles that determines our fate, but rather how we choose to confront and overcome them. The best approach to tackling challenges and obstacles in execution involves a combination of resilience, adaptability, and strategic planning.

Resilience is the cornerstone of overcoming challenges. It is the ability to bounce back from setbacks, to maintain a positive outlook in the face of adversity, and to persevere in the pursuit of our goals. Cultivating resilience involves developing a growth mindset, reframing setbacks as opportunities for learning and growth, and drawing on inner strength and determination to keep moving forward. By embracing resilience, we can navigate through challenges with a sense of purpose and determination, ultimately emerging stronger and more capable.

Adaptability is another crucial element in overcoming obstacles. In a rapidly changing world, the ability to adapt to new circumstances and unforeseen challenges is essential for success. This requires a willingness to embrace change, to think creatively, and to be open to new ideas and approaches. By remaining flexible and adaptable, we can adjust our strategies in response to unexpected obstacles, finding innovative solutions that enable us to move past roadblocks and continue making progress.

Strategic planning is the third pillar of the best approach to overcoming challenges in execution. While resilience and adaptability provide the foundation for navigating obstacles, strategic planning empowers us to anticipate potential challenges and proactively address them. This involves setting clear goals, breaking them down into manageable steps, and identifying potential risks and barriers along the way. By developing a well-thought-out plan, we can mitigate potential obstacles before they arise, allowing us to execute our initiatives with greater efficiency and confidence.

In conclusion, overcoming challenges and obstacles in execution requires a multi-faceted approach that encompasses resilience, adaptability, and strategic planning. By cultivating resilience, we can weather setbacks and maintain our momentum in the face of adversity. By embracing adaptability, we can respond to unforeseen challenges with creativity and flexibility. And by implementing strategic planning, we can anticipate potential obstacles and chart a clear path toward our goals. With this holistic approach, we can confront challenges head-on, navigate through obstacles, and ultimately achieve success in our endeavors.

Chapter 5: Entrepreneurial Execution Mastery

5.1 Applying Entrepreneurial Mindset to Execute Big Ideas

In the realm of entrepreneurship, the ability to execute big ideas is often the differentiating factor between success and failure. While having a visionary concept is essential, it is the execution of that idea that truly determines its impact. In this chapter, we will explore how applying an entrepreneurial mindset can be the key to effectively executing big ideas, and we will delve into the "how" and "when" of leveraging this mindset for maximum impact.

The entrepreneurial mindset is characterized by a unique blend of creativity, resilience, and a willingness to take calculated risks. When it comes to executing big ideas, this mindset becomes a powerful tool for turning vision into reality. By embracing creativity, entrepreneurs can think outside the box, envisioning innovative solutions to complex problems and identifying new opportunities for growth. This creative approach is essential for executing big ideas, as it allows entrepreneurs to see possibilities where others see obstacles and to craft unique strategies for bringing their visions to life.

Resilience is another hallmark of the entrepreneurial mindset, and it is crucial for executing big ideas in the face of challenges and setbacks. The road to bringing a big idea to fruition is rarely smooth, and entrepreneurs must be prepared to weather adversity with determination and unwavering resolve. By maintaining a positive outlook in the face of obstacles, entrepreneurs can overcome setbacks and stay the course, ultimately achieving success through their resilience and perseverance.

Taking calculated risks is also a fundamental aspect of the entrepreneurial mindset that is essential for executing big ideas. Entrepreneurs must be willing to step outside their comfort zones, make bold decisions, and embrace uncertainty in pursuit of their visions. By carefully assessing potential risks and rewards, entrepreneurs can make informed choices that propel their big ideas forward, seizing opportunities and navigating through challenges with confidence.

The "how" and "when" of applying the entrepreneurial mindset to execute big ideas are critical considerations. Entrepreneurs should leverage this mindset from the very inception of their ventures, infusing their strategic planning and decision-making processes with creativity, resilience, and a willingness to take calculated risks. This means actively seeking out new opportunities, embracing change, and constantly refining their strategies to align with their overarching vision.

Furthermore, **the entrepreneurial mindset should be continuously nurtured throughout the execution phase**, serving as a guiding force that empowers entrepreneurs to adapt to unforeseen challenges, pivot when necessary, and remain steadfast in their pursuit of their big ideas.

In conclusion, applying an entrepreneurial mindset is essential for executing big ideas with impact. By embracing creativity, resilience, and a willingness to take calculated risks, entrepreneurs can navigate through obstacles, capitalize on opportunities, and ultimately bring their visionary concepts to fruition. This mindset should be ingrained in every stage of the entrepreneurial journey, from ideation to execution, ensuring that big ideas are not just imagined but realized with purpose and determination.

5.2 Leveraging Innovation and Creativity in Business Execution

In today's dynamic and competitive business landscape, the ability to leverage innovation and creativity is a crucial element in achieving entrepreneurial execution mastery. By infusing these qualities into the execution of business strategies, entrepreneurs can differentiate themselves, drive growth, and create sustainable success. Let's explore how innovation and creativity can be harnessed to propel business execution to new heights.

Embracing innovation is essential for staying ahead of the curve in a rapidly evolving marketplace. Entrepreneurs who prioritize innovation in their execution strategies are better positioned to disrupt industries, introduce groundbreaking products or services, and meet the ever-changing needs of their customers. By fostering a culture of innovation within their organizations, entrepreneurs can encourage their teams to think outside the box, experiment with new ideas, and continuously push the boundaries of what is possible.

Moreover, creativity plays a pivotal role in business execution by enabling entrepreneurs to envision unconventional solutions to complex challenges. When creativity is infused into the execution process, entrepreneurs can devise unique approaches to problem-solving, product development, and market expansion. By tapping into their creative instincts, entrepreneurs can uncover opportunities that others may overlook and craft strategies that set their ventures apart from the competition.

To leverage innovation and creativity effectively in business execution, entrepreneurs should foster an environment that encourages experimentation and risk-taking. This entails empowering their teams to explore new concepts, challenge existing norms, and embrace a mindset of continuous improvement. By creating a safe space for innovation and creativity, entrepreneurs can unlock the full potential of their teams and inspire them to contribute fresh ideas that drive the execution of business strategies forward.

Furthermore, entrepreneurs can harness the power of cross-functional collaboration to fuel innovation and creativity in business execution. By bringing together diverse perspectives from different departments and disciplines, entrepreneurs can spark new ideas, gain valuable insights, and develop comprehensive execution plans that leverage the collective expertise of their teams.

In conclusion, leveraging innovation and creativity is instrumental in achieving entrepreneurial execution mastery. By prioritizing these qualities in business execution, entrepreneurs can drive meaningful change, differentiate their ventures, and carve out a lasting impact in their respective industries. Through a commitment to fostering innovation, embracing creativity, and nurturing a collaborative environment, entrepreneurs can unlock new possibilities and propel their businesses to unprecedented levels of success.

Chapter 6 Achieving Ambitious Business Goals.

6.1 Setting and Attaining Stretch Goals through Effective Execution

In the pursuit of ambitious business goals, setting and attaining stretch goals through effective execution is a transformative approach that empowers entrepreneurs to surpass conventional limits and achieve extraordinary outcomes. By embracing stretch goals—audacious objectives that push the boundaries of what is deemed achievable—entrepreneurs can propel their ventures to new heights of success. Let's look at how the strategic alignment of stretch goals with effective execution can drive unprecedented business performance and foster a culture of relentless innovation.

The process of setting stretch goals begins with a bold vision that challenges the status quo and ignites a sense of purpose within the organization. By articulating a compelling vision that embodies audacious aspirations, entrepreneurs can inspire their teams to strive for greatness and rally behind a shared commitment to realizing the extraordinary. This visionary perspective serves as the catalyst for setting stretch goals that demand exceptional performance, creativity, and perseverance.

Moreover, effective execution is the key element that transforms stretch goals from aspirational targets into tangible achievements. Entrepreneurs must cultivate a disciplined approach to execution that encompasses meticulous planning, resource allocation, and relentless focus on driving progress. By aligning every facet of their organization with the pursuit of stretch goals, entrepreneurs can instill a sense of urgency, accountability, and resilience that propels their teams toward the realization of audacious aspirations.

To attain stretch goals through effective execution, entrepreneurs must foster a culture of innovation, agility, and continuous improvement within their organizations. This entails empowering their teams to embrace calculated risks, experiment with novel approaches, and adapt swiftly to changing dynamics. By fostering an environment that encourages bold experimentation and learning from setbacks, entrepreneurs can position their ventures to conquer uncharted territory and achieve breakthrough results.

Furthermore, the strategic deployment of resources and capabilities is essential in driving the effective execution of stretch goals. Entrepreneurs must allocate resources judiciously, leverage their core competencies, and forge strategic partnerships that amplify their capacity to tackle formidable challenges. By orchestrating the optimal utilization of resources in alignment with stretch goals, entrepreneurs can maximize their ability to surmount obstacles and capitalize on emerging opportunities.

In conclusion, setting and attaining stretch goals through effective execution is a pivotal driver of entrepreneurial success. By anchoring their organizations in a visionary perspective, cultivating a disciplined approach to execution, fostering a culture of innovation, and strategically deploying resources, entrepreneurs can transcend conventional boundaries and accomplish remarkable feats. Through the pursuit of stretch goals, entrepreneurs can unleash the full potential of their ventures and leave an indelible mark on their industries.

6.2 Strategies for Sustaining Momentum and Achieving Long-Term Success

In the dynamic landscape of business, sustaining momentum and achieving long-term success is a multifaceted endeavor that demands strategic foresight, adaptability, and unwavering dedication. To navigate the complexities of the modern marketplace and carve a path to enduring prosperity, entrepreneurs must embrace a holistic approach that encompasses innovative strategies, agile leadership, and a relentless commitment to excellence. Let's explore the pivotal strategies that entrepreneurs can leverage to sustain momentum and achieve long-term success in their ventures.

1. **Cultivate a Culture of Innovation**:
At the heart of sustaining momentum and achieving long-term success lies a culture of innovation that thrives on creativity, forward thinking, and a willingness to challenge the status quo. Entrepreneurs must foster an environment where novel ideas are encouraged, risk-taking is embraced, and continuous improvement is ingrained in the organizational ethos. By nurturing a culture of innovation, entrepreneurs can infuse their ventures with the agility and adaptability needed to stay ahead of the curve and drive sustained growth.

2. **Embrace Strategic Agility:**
In an ever-evolving business landscape, strategic agility is indispensable for sustaining momentum and achieving long-term success. Entrepreneurs must be adept at swiftly adapting to market shifts, technological advancements, and changing consumer preferences. By embracing strategic agility, entrepreneurs can pivot their strategies, reallocate resources, and capitalize on emerging opportunities with precision and speed, thereby fortifying their ventures against obsolescence and positioning them for sustained relevance.

3. **Prioritize Customer-Centricity**:
Sustaining momentum and achieving long-term success hinges on a deep understanding of customer needs, preferences, and expectations. Entrepreneurs must prioritize customer-centricity by actively engaging with their clientele, soliciting feedback, and tailoring their offerings to deliver exceptional value. By placing the

customer at the center of their operations, entrepreneurs can build enduring relationships, foster brand loyalty, and sustain momentum through a loyal customer base that propels sustained growth.

4. **Foster Strategic Partnerships:**
Collaborative partnerships with like-minded organizations can be instrumental in sustaining momentum and achieving long-term success. Entrepreneurs should seek out strategic alliances that complement their strengths, expand their reach, and unlock new avenues for growth. By forging symbiotic partnerships, entrepreneurs can leverage collective expertise, shared resources, and mutual support to navigate challenges, capitalize on synergies, and propel their ventures toward sustained success.

5. **Invest in Talent Development:**
A robust talent pool is a cornerstone of sustained success. Entrepreneurs must invest in talent development by nurturing a high-performance culture, providing ongoing training and mentorship, and empowering their teams to unleash their full potential. By cultivating a skilled and motivated workforce, entrepreneurs can fuel innovation, drive operational excellence, and sustain momentum through the collective capabilities of their human capital.

In conclusion, sustaining momentum and achieving long-term success necessitates a strategic confluence of innovation, agility, customer-centricity, strategic partnerships, and talent development. By embracing these foundational strategies, entrepreneurs can chart a course toward enduring prosperity, fortify their ventures against disruption, and leave an indelible mark on their industries. With unwavering dedication to these principles, entrepreneurs can sustain momentum and realize the vision of long-term success for their ventures.

Chapter 7. Mindset Shifts for Business Success.

7.1 Cultivating a Mindset of Execution Excellence

In the realm of business success, the cultivation of a mindset centered on execution excellence is a transformative imperative that empowers entrepreneurs to transcend obstacles, drive meaningful progress, and actualize their vision with unwavering precision. At its core, a mindset of execution excellence embodies a resolute commitment to action, an unwavering focus on results, and a relentless pursuit of operational mastery. By embracing this paradigm shift, entrepreneurs can unleash the full potential of their ventures and propel them toward sustained success. Let's take a look at examine the foundational principles and actionable strategies for cultivating a mindset of execution excellence.

1. Embrace a Bias for Action:

A mindset of execution excellence is underpinned by a bias for action—a proactive orientation that eschews complacency and inertia in favor of decisive, purposeful movement. Entrepreneurs must cultivate a sense of urgency, an appetite for calculated risk-taking, and a willingness to swiftly translate ideas into tangible outcomes. By embracing a bias for action, entrepreneurs can infuse their ventures with momentum, drive impactful change, and outmaneuver the inertia that stifles progress.

2. **Foster a Results-Driven Focus:**
Central to a mindset of execution excellence is a relentless focus on results—a steadfast commitment to delivering outcomes that surpass expectations and propel the venture forward. Entrepreneurs must instill a results-driven culture that prioritizes accountability, measures performance against clear objectives, and celebrates tangible achievements. By fostering a results-driven focus, entrepreneurs can align their teams toward common goals, galvanize collective effort, and elevate the standard of excellence across their organizations.

3. **Cultivate Operational Discipline:**
Execution excellence hinges on the cultivation of operational discipline—a systematic approach to planning, resource allocation, and flawless execution. Entrepreneurs must instill rigorous processes, optimize workflows, and eliminate inefficiencies to ensure seamless implementation of strategic initiatives. By cultivating operational discipline, entrepreneurs can mitigate risks, enhance productivity, and fortify their ventures with the resilience needed to navigate complexities and deliver consistent results.

4. **Embody Adaptive Leadership:**
A mindset of execution excellence demands adaptive leadership—an agile, forward-thinking approach that

empowers entrepreneurs to navigate uncertainty, embrace change, and steer their ventures toward success amidst evolving landscapes. Entrepreneurs must embody resilience, inspire confidence in their teams, and pivot strategies with acumen to seize opportunities and overcome challenges. By embodying adaptive leadership, entrepreneurs can instill a culture of agility, drive innovation, and sustain momentum through astute decision-making and nimble course corrections.

In conclusion, cultivating a mindset of execution excellence is an indispensable catalyst for propelling ventures toward enduring success. By embracing a bias for action, fostering a results-driven focus, cultivating operational discipline, and embodying adaptive leadership, entrepreneurs can harness the transformative power of execution excellence to surmount barriers, drive sustained progress, and realize the full potential of their ventures. With an unwavering commitment to these principles, entrepreneurs can elevate their operational prowess and carve a path toward lasting success in the dynamic landscape of business.

7.2 Overcoming Mental Barriers to Achieve Big Things in Business

In the pursuit of business success, the ability to overcome mental barriers is a transformative imperative that empowers entrepreneurs to transcend limitations, unlock their full potential, and achieve remarkable feats. At its core, this journey requires a profound mindset shift—one that dismantles self-imposed constraints, cultivates resilience, and fosters an unwavering belief in one's ability to achieve big things. Let's explore the pivotal mindset shifts that entrepreneurs can embrace to conquer mental barriers and unleash their capacity for extraordinary success.

1. Embrace a Growth Mindset:
Overcoming mental barriers begins with embracing a growth mindset—a belief that talents and abilities can be developed through dedication and hard work. Entrepreneurs must shift from a fixed mindset, which is constrained by self-doubt and fear of failure, to a growth mindset that thrives on challenges, sees setbacks as opportunities for growth, and sustains a passion for learning. By cultivating a growth mindset, entrepreneurs can break free from the shackles of self-limiting beliefs and unleash their innate potential to achieve remarkable success.

2. **Harness the Power of Resilience:**
Conquering mental barriers necessitates harnessing the power of resilience—an unwavering determination to persevere in the face of adversity, setbacks, and uncertainty. Entrepreneurs must cultivate an indomitable spirit, embrace failure as a stepping stone to success, and view challenges as opportunities to demonstrate resilience and fortitude. By building resilience, entrepreneurs can weather the storms of entrepreneurship, bounce back from setbacks, and forge ahead with unwavering resolve toward their most audacious goals.

3. **Foster a Fearless Mindset:**
To achieve big things in business, entrepreneurs must foster a fearless mindset—a bold, audacious approach that confronts fears, takes calculated risks, and embraces discomfort as a catalyst for growth. Entrepreneurs must silence the inner voice of doubt, confront fear of failure head-on, and boldly pursue ambitious endeavors with unwavering confidence. By fostering a fearless mindset, entrepreneurs can break free from the constraints of comfort zones, seize opportunities with conviction, and propel their ventures toward extraordinary achievements.

4. **Cultivate a Positive Self-Image:**
Overcoming mental barriers necessitates cultivating a positive self-image—a deep sense of self-worth, confidence, and belief in one's ability to achieve

greatness. Entrepreneurs must banish self-doubt, embrace their unique strengths and talents, and foster a positive internal dialogue that fuels courage and conviction. By cultivating a positive self-image, entrepreneurs can exude confidence, inspire trust in others, and project an unwavering belief in their capacity to achieve big things in business.

In conclusion, overcoming mental barriers is an essential journey that empowers entrepreneurs to unleash their full potential and achieve remarkable success in the dynamic landscape of business. By embracing a growth mindset, harnessing the power of resilience, fostering a fearless mindset, and cultivating a positive self-image, entrepreneurs can transcend mental barriers and carve a path toward extraordinary achievements that redefine the boundaries of success. With these transformative mindset shifts, entrepreneurs can unlock their capacity for greatness and propel their ventures toward enduring success.

Conclusion

In conclusion, "The Power of Execution: Getting Big Things Done in Business" illuminates the transformative imperative of overcoming mental barriers to achieve remarkable success. Through the lens of this book, entrepreneurs are empowered to embrace a growth mindset, harness the power of resilience, foster a fearless mindset, and cultivate a positive self-image. These pivotal mindset shifts serve as the cornerstone for unlocking one's full potential and propelling ventures toward enduring success.

As the final pages of this book turn, a call to action resounds with unwavering conviction. It beckons entrepreneurs to seize the reins of their destinies, confront self-imposed limitations, and embark on a journey of audacious execution. It implores them to embrace challenges as opportunities for growth, view setbacks as stepping stones to success, and forge ahead with unyielding determination. The call to action echoes the resounding truth that greatness lies within reach, awaiting those bold enough to grasp it.

Now is the time for entrepreneurs to rise above the fray, shatter the glass ceiling of self-doubt, and unleash their capacity for extraordinary achievements. As the final chapter closes, the call to action resounds with clarity: Go forth with courage, tenacity, and an unwavering belief in your ability to execute big things in business. The power to achieve greatness lies within your grasp—seize it with unrelenting resolve and write your own story of triumph.

May this book serve as a beacon of inspiration and empowerment, propelling entrepreneurs toward a future defined by audacious execution and enduring success. The time for action is now—embrace the power of execution and unleash your potential to achieve big things in business.

Recap of Key Insights and Actionable Steps for Getting Big Things Done in Business

In the fast-paced world of business, the power of execution is essential for achieving big things. Here's a recap of key insights and actionable steps to drive successful business execution:

1. Clear Vision and Strategy: Start by defining a clear vision and strategy for your business. This provides a roadmap for achieving your goals and ensures that

everyone in the organization is aligned towards a common purpose.

2. Effective Planning: Break down big goals into smaller, manageable tasks. Create a detailed plan with specific milestones and deadlines to keep the team focused and on track.

3. Empower Your Team: Surround yourself with talented individuals and empower them to take ownership of their responsibilities. Encourage collaboration and open communication to foster a culture of accountability and innovation.

4. Adaptability: In today's dynamic business environment, adaptability is key. Be open to change, embrace new ideas, and be willing to pivot when necessary to stay ahead of the curve.

5. Measure Progress: Implement key performance indicators (KPIs) to track progress and make data-driven decisions. Regularly review performance metrics to identify areas for improvement and celebrate successes.

6. Execution Excellence: Strive for excellence in execution by paying attention to detail, maintaining high standards, and continuously seeking ways to optimize processes.

By applying these insights and taking actionable steps, businesses can overcome challenges, capitalize on opportunities, and achieve big things through effective execution. Remember, the power of execution lies in the ability to turn vision into reality through strategic planning, empowered teams, adaptability, and a relentless pursuit of excellence.